Hyd

The Definitive Begir
Growing Vegetables, Fruits, & Herbs for Self-
Sufficiency!

MICHAEL MARTINEZ

© Copyright 2015 - All rights reserved.

In no way is it legal to reproduce, duplicate, or transmit any part of this document in either electronic means or in printed format. Recording of this publication is strictly prohibited and any storage of this document is not allowed unless with written permission from the publisher. All rights reserved.

The information provided herein is stated to be truthful and consistent, in that any liability, in terms of inattention or otherwise, by any usage or abuse of any policies, processes, or directions contained within is the solitary and utter responsibility of the recipient reader. Under no circumstances will any legal responsibility or blame be held against the publisher for any reparation, damages, or monetary loss due to the information herein, either directly or indirectly.

Respective authors own all copyrights not held by the publisher.

Legal Notice:
This book is copyright protected. This is only for personal use. You cannot amend, distribute, sell, use, quote or paraphrase any part or the content within this book without the consent of the author or copyright owner. Legal action will be pursued if this is breached.

Disclaimer Notice:
Please note the information contained within this document is for educational and entertainment purposes only. Every attempt has been made to provide accurate, up to date and reliable complete information. No warranties of any kind are expressed or implied. Readers acknowledge that the author is not engaging in the rendering of legal, financial, medical or professional advice.

By reading this document, the reader agrees that under no circumstances are we responsible for any losses, direct or indirect, which are incurred as a result of the use of information contained within this document, including, but not limited to, —errors, omissions, or inaccuracies.

Table of Contents

Introduction 7

Chapter 1: Hydroponics: An Overview 8
Why Plants Are Grown in Soil 8
A Timeline of the Development of the Hydroponics System 8

Chapter 2: Hydroponics vs. Soil Gardening 11

Chapter 3: Choosing a Hydroponic System 14
Types of Hydroponic Systems 14
Basic Parts of a Hydroponic Growing System 16

Chapter 4: Starting a Hydroponic Garden 20
Building Your Own Hydroponic Growing System (Drip Method) 20

Chapter 5: Fruits - A Growing Cheat Sheet 27
Popular Fruits 27

Chapter 6: Vegetables - A Growing Cheat Sheet 33
General Growing Tips 33

Chapter 7: Herbs – A Growing Cheat Sheet 38
Benefits of Growing Herbs 38
General Growing Tips 39
Saving Herbs 41

Chapter 8: Planning Your Garden 43

Chapter 9: Water Maintenance, Garden Expansion, and More: Tips from the Experts on Hydroponics 47
Water Maintenance 47
Garden Expansion 48
Important Maintenance Tips 51
Adding nutrients 53

Chapter 10: Common Mistakes Newbies Make 55
Starting Your Garden without Proper Knowledge 55
Harvesting too Early 55
Overwatering/Under Watering 56
Improper Lighting 56
Ignoring pH 56

Overfeeding the Plants 57
Insufficient Air Circulation 57
Unhygienic Conditions 58
Falling into the Cheap Trap 58
Pest Control via Plants 59

Chapter 11: Troubleshooting Your Hydroponics Garden 59
Troubleshooting Issue #1: The Lighting 59
Troubleshooting Issue #2: The Growing Climate 61
Troubleshooting Issue #3: The Nutrient System 61
Troubleshooting Issue #4: Pests 62
Troubleshooting Issue #5: Gross Coatings (Not From Bugs) 66
Troubleshooting Issue #6: The Leaves 69
Other Troubleshooting Problems 70

Conclusion 72

Introduction

Have you ever questioned what you would do to feed yourself in the event of an economic crash or a catastrophic event that wiped out food stores? How would you sustain yourself and how would you make sure that your family could eat? There is a very simple answer to these questions—agricultural hydroponics.

Thank you for downloading this book, *Hydroponics: The Definitive Beginner's Guide to Quickly Start Growing Vegetables, Fruits, & Herbs for Self-Sufficiency!*

Hydroponics is a type of growing process that is accomplished without using soil. It involves the use of nutrient-rich water and one of several techniques to help the plant intake various nutrients it needs for growth. It has a number of benefits over more traditional growing methods, which you will learn in this book.

In this book, you are going to learn the history of hydroponics and why it is a good growing method. You will also learn the techniques used for hydroponics and how to get started. Finally, you will learn how to troubleshoot your hydroponic growing system if it is not working right.

Whether you are interested in hydroponic growing as a relaxing hobby or you are trying to teach yourself the important art of self-sustainment, this book will teach you everything that you need to know to get started with hydroponics. Learn this useful and relaxing skill today.

Best of luck!

Chapter 1: Hydroponics: An Overview

Hydroponics is a means of growing plants without soil. It makes use of nutrient-rich water, or a nutrient solution as well as techniques that allow the plant to grow. You can also use sand or gravel, with added nutrients. In this chapter, you are going to learn the history of the growing art that we call hydroponics. You will also learn about some of its practical uses throughout history.

Why Plants Are Grown in Soil

Traditionally, soil is used to grow plants. It was thought that soil was necessary, since plants started out in the earth, with nutrient rich soils like the strawberry plants that were first grown in the wild before being cultivated for gardens. At some point in history, it was discovered that the soil was not necessary for the growing process. Rather, the role of soil is to act as a reservoir to hold the nutrients that a plant needs in order to grow.

A Timeline of the Development of the Hydroponics System

It was 1627 when the idea of hydroponics was published, in *Sylva Sylvarum* by Francis Bacon. While he would not be around to see it, (he died the year before *Sylva Sylvarum* was published) Sir Francis Bacon had established the idea of water culture, which would be explored for centuries before arriving at the systems used today.

John Woodward was the next man to study the growth of plants using water culture. He published a study of his experiments in 1699, for which he used spearmints. There would be a number of other studies done after this one until a list of the nine essential nutrients for plant growth was compiled in 1842. Finally, between the years of 1859 and 1875, the soilless cultivation technique that is known as hydroponics was developed. German botanists Wilhelm Knop and Julius von Sachs were credited the modern design system for hydroponics.

It would be 1929 before hydroponics would be considered for the production of agricultural crops. William Frederick Gericke initially called this process aquaculture, but it was dropped after he learned that aquaculture was already used to describe the culturing of aquatic organisms. W. A. Setchell suggested the term hydroponics in 1937 and it stuck.

Gericke was a student at the University of California at Berkeley and was originally denied use of the on-ground greenhouses for his study. After he had successfully grown 25-foot tall tomato plants in nutrient-filled solution, however, the University petitioned him for to use the solution in their greenhouses. He again requested access to greenhouses and research facilities, which the University approved. Still, his ideas were met with skepticism. The University requested two other students investigate his claim. Daniel Arnon, and Dennis Hoagland investigated Gericke's research and reported their findings in an agriculture bulletin in 1938, titled *The Water Culture Method for Growing Plants Without Soil*. At first they missed several advantages of agricultural hydroponics when compared against traditional agricultural methods. However, Hoagland eventually developed several mineral nutrient solutions. There are still several altered versions of these original methods (called Hoagland solutions) used today.

Practical Uses of Hydroponic Growing Systems Throughout History

It was in the 1930s that the most well-known early success with the agricultural hydroponics method occurred. There was a soilless island in the Pacific Ocean called Wake Island. It was used as a refueling stop for Pan American airline, though it had one major problem: the lack of soil meant that the airline had to airlift vegetables for passengers to eat, which could be incredibly expensive.

So, what was the solution? Hydroponics. Vegetables were grown for the passengers for a price significantly lower than it cost to airlift vegetables to the island.

There have also been a number of other practical applications of hydroponics in the twentieth and twenty-first centuries. These include:

- Walt Disney World's EPCOT Center has an area called The Land Pavilion, where a number of hydroponic techniques have been used to grow food since the early 1980s.

- NASA has considered hydroponic growing areas to sustain life in space, as well as on Mars.

Now that you have a brief understanding of how we arrived at the growing system that is called hydroponics, it is time to learn the many benefits and how you can grow your own fruits, vegetables, and herbs at home.

Chapter 2: Hydroponics vs. Soil Gardening

So, what makes hydroponics so different from traditional soil gardening methods? In this chapter, you are going to find out. Here are the advantages of each type of plant growing concept.

Areas Where Hydroponic Gardening is Better

- **Hydroponics prevents the overuse of fertilizer.** Hydroponic plants are grown in a very controlled environment, where waste products are limited and less nutrient material is needed. The great thing about this control is that it allows less fertilizer to be used. This is especially beneficial for the humans and animals in the area, who will have less of a chance of drinking fertilizer-contaminated water.

- **Hydroponics make better use of space and location.** You can grow an indoor hydroponics system anywhere that you have room, because it takes up so little space and everything that the plant needs can be provided by your system. Additionally, roots grown in the soil need room to spread out while plants grown hydroponically have root systems that do not need to spread out. This means that you can grow plants closer together and save space.

- **Hydroponics uses less water.** You would think that a hydroponic growing system would use more water than traditional methods, but that is not true. When plants are grown hydroponically, they are given only the amount of water that they need. When you water plants that are in soil, some of the water is going to seep into the ground or leak out of the pot. It will also be evaporated. Therefore, the plants are actually receiving only a fraction of the water that you are providing. Hydroponic systems are much more efficient when it comes to water usage and you actually end up using 70 to 80 percent less water.

- **Hydroponics systems reduce weeds, pests, and diseases.** When you use more traditional gardening methods, the soil that you grow in can be filled with diseases, pests, and other plant parts. Hydroponic systems do away with this problem almost entirely.

- **Hydroponic systems grow plants twice as fast as traditional methods.** Do you know what that means? You can have more harvests each year. Because hydroponic systems provide exactly what the plant needs without the plant having to hunt for it, the growing cycle is much more efficient.

- **Hydroponics makes it easier for you to tamper with the nutrients for growing.** Every plant, like every person, is unique. Each type is going to thrive in certain environments and struggle in others. Hydroponics is fun in this way. You have the ability to adjust the amount of nutrients in the solution and adjust it until you have the perfect growth solution.

Areas Where Soil Gardening is Better

- **Soil gardening has a lower initial cost.** While hydroponics systems vary in their initial cost, they can get quite expensive. Some of this cost will be offset by the lesser amount of water, fertilizer, and pesticides that you will need.

- **Soil gardening does not use electricity.** In several hydroponics gardening techniques, you must use a light source. Additionally, some systems use electricity to create bubbles in the nutrient system to aerate the roots.

- **Soil gardening has a less risk of mold and bacteria growth.** One disadvantage of hydroponics is that plants are grown in a very moist environment. This leaves the plants susceptible to growth of mold and sometimes dangerous bacteria if enough precautions are not taken.

Now that you have an understanding of the major ways that hydroponics differs from more traditional growing methods using soil, it is time to move on. In the next chapter, we will discuss the various types of hydroponic systems available and how to choose the best system for your home garden.

Chapter 3: Choosing a Hydroponic System

As the field of agricultural hydroponics has been studied, there are numerous systems that have been evaluated for effectiveness. In this chapter, you will learn about the different types of hydroponics systems and the techniques that can be used so you can grow your own garden for self-sufficiency.

Types of Hydroponic Systems

There are six major types of hydroponic growing system. There are altered versions of these, some systems combine two or more techniques, but all hydroponic systems are derived from one of these six major types.

Drip System

The drip system is recovery or non-recovery in design. They are also the most popular type of system used around the world. The operation of the drip system is based on a timer control with a submersed pump. The pump is turned on with the timer and the nutrient solution is allowed to drip onto the base of each plant via a small drip line. With a recovery system the nutrient excess will run off and collect in a reservoir to be re-used. The non-recovery system does not collect the run-off. The recovery system is more efficient, since you re-use the nutrients rather than collecting the waste. You also save money on the setup since the watering cycle does not need an expensive timer to provide precise control of the amount of nutrients sent to the plants. However, a non-recovery system requires less maintenance, since you do not have to monitor the pH of the reservoir and thus the re-used nutrients.

Nutrient Film Technique (NFT)

For the nutrient film technique (NFT) you need a reservoir, a pump, and a growing tray that is placed at a tilt. A pump is placed in the reservoir to circulate the nutrient through a tube and up to the growing tray. The nutrient runs down the growing tray, where the roots are dangling down. Because the tray is at an angle, the extra nutrient solution runs down back into the reservoir tank.

Water Culture

For a water culture system, you will need an air pump to keep the roots of your plant adequately oxygenated. The reservoir and the growing chamber are essentially the same part. The roots of the plant will be submerged completely by the nutrient solution, which is the reason that an air pump is needed.

Ebb-Flow (also referred to as Flood & Drain)

The ebb-flow hydroponic system uses a submersible pump to pump the nutrient solution between the reservoir and the grow tray. When there is too much nutrient solution in the grow tray, the excess will flow back down into the reservoir. This makes for very efficient use of nutrient solution.

Wick System

The wick system is one of the simplest setups. In fact, you may want to consider this as you build your own hydroponics systems. Basically, a wick runs from the growing tray with the plants to the reservoir. The nutrient solution is kept in the reservoir and the wick will pull it up whenever the plant roots need it.

Aeroponics

The basic setup of an Aeroponics system makes use of a drip sprayer. The roots of the plant are suspended in the grow chamber, hanging in the air. The drip sprayer is set up on a timer and the plant roots are misted with the nutrient system as often as necessary.

Considerations

There are several things that you should consider before deciding which hydroponics system is right for you, including:

- The plant(s) that you are growing
    - Root size
    - Amount of water and oxygen needed by the roots
    - Size of the full grown plant
- How easy it is to take apart to clean between growing cycles
- How easy/difficult it is to repair
- The number and types of plants that you want to plant

Basic Parts of a Hydroponic Growing System

If you are trying to go the professional route, there are hydroponic growing systems that can be bought for hundreds, or even thousands of dollars. However, you can also choose to build your own growing system. In order to do that, you need an understanding of what basic parts make up a hydroponic growing system.

Growing Tray/Chamber

The growing chamber or growing tray is the area where the roots of your plants are going to grow. This is meant to allow the roots to access the nutrient system and support the plants. The type(s) of plants that you are growing will determine the shape and size of growing container that is going to work best.

As you are choosing the materials for your growing chamber, be sure to choose something that will prevent the roots from being exposed to light. It should also protect your fruits, vegetables, and herbs from high temperatures, pests, and mold growth.

Reservoir

The reservoir is responsible for holding the nutrient solution that your plants need to grow. It works in different ways depending on the system that you use. Some hydroponics systems use the reservoir as part of the growing chamber by allowing the roots to hang in the reservoir constantly. Other systems may use a system that pumps the solution from the reservoir into the growing tray on a timer.

The best material for a reservoir is plastic. It holds water and is easy to clean, so you can use almost any container. One thing to remember, however, is that the reservoir material you use must be opaque. You should not be able to see light shining through. If necessary, wrap the plastic container that you are using with newspaper or bubble wrap, or paint it. This is essential to prevent the growth of algae and microorganisms in your nutrient solution.

Delivery System

The delivery system is essential to get the nutrient solution from the reservoir to the roots of your plant. It can be simple plumbing made out of PVC tubing and connectors or include sprayers or drip emitters. One thing to remember is that if you choose extras like a sprayer or drip emitter, they are highly susceptible to clogging. You will want to make sure you have extra parts on hand for replacement as you clean the hardware.

Grow Lights

Not all hydroponics systems will require a grow light. If you are growing out of season, however, or if the location in your home does not support natural sunlight, then a grow light is necessary to grow plants hydroponically. When you choose a grow light, be sure you are choosing one specifically for growing plants. Other types of lighting do not emit the right frequency of light that is necessary for your plant to undergo photosynthesis.

Timer

In order for your plant to grow, it will need nutrients and sunlight set on a schedule that encourages growth. You will need 1-2 timers for your hydroponics kit. The first is to control the on/off pump that is necessary to aerate your roof. The second will control any artificial light you are using, if any.

Pump

There are two types of pumps used for hydroponics growing systems- the submersible pump and the air pump.

The submersible pump is often a pond or fountain pump. These are used to pump the nutrient solution from the reservoir to the growing chamber. Make sure that you choose the size that is appropriate for your growing setup. Also, be sure to clean the pump (and its filter) regularly so that it is pumping your nutrient system into your growing tray and nothing else.

Air pumps are used to create an air supply for the roots of your plant. Unless you are using a water culture system, the use of an air pump is optional. However, they are fairly inexpensive, so it is a good investment. The reason that it is necessary for water culture systems is because the roots are submerged in the solution 24/7 and it is necessary to get air to the roots. When used in a system other than a water culture system, air pumps keep the water in the reservoir oxygenated. Some of the other benefits of an air pump include keeping the nutrients and water mixed well and reduced likelihood of pathogens in the reservoir.

The drip system can be started for around $100, if you have a small budget. Now that you know what types of systems are out there and the major components that you need, we will discuss how to build a hydroponics growing system.

Chapter 4: Starting a Hydroponic Garden

It is very easy to start a hydroponic garden at home. Follow the instructions in this chapter, and you will learn how. If you want advice about growing specific plants in your garden, sit tight! We will discuss tips for growing the best fruits, vegetables, and herbs in the next chapter.

Building Your Own Hydroponic Growing System (Drip Method)

If you do not have hundreds or thousands of dollars to spend on a growing system from the store, you can easily make your own system at home. This section will teach you to build a drip-style hydroponic growing system. This particular system can be built for $60-$100, depending on where you buy your materials from.

Materials

You will need:

- 4- Five gallon buckets
- 4 Bulkhead fittings (thread nuts)
- Submersible fountain pump
- Furnace filter
- Black (or blue) vinyl tubing for the fill and drain lines
- "T" Connectors that will fit your vinyl tubing
- 18 to 30-gallon storage tote (this will be your reservoir- bigger is better!)

- Rocks (Rinse, soak for an hour in 1-part bleach to 10 parts water and then rinse again)

- Growing medium (such as clay balls, Perlite, or Coconut Coir)

- Spray paint- 2 cans black and 2 cans white

- 15 Amp Timer

Other Supplies

The other things that you will need include:

- Hydroponic growth nutrients (you can make your own blend if you know what you are doing)

- pH testing kit

- pH adjusters to raise or lower the pH after testing

- Rotary tool, hot metal, or something else to cut/burn/burr holes into the plastic bucket (make sure you can get the edges smooth)

- Electrical tape

- Heat source (lighter)

- Paper clip

Instructions

Before building your drip hydroponic system, you need to consider where you will be placing it. It will determine if you need more materials, such as a grow light, plastic, or bench to set your system on. The plants will grow up from the top of the open bucket, but you also have to have a drainage system in the bottom of the bucket for excess nutrients. The buckets cannot sit on the ground of a green house, backyard, or other area. Your plants are also going to need sunlight to grow, since hydroponics still require photosynthesis for the plants to be healthy and bear fruit or vegetables.

If you have a small budget, you may consider using a patio table you already have or buying 2x4s to build a bench to raise your buckets off of the ground.

1. Begin by tracing a hole in the bottom of the bucket, using the nut from the bulkhead fittings as your guidance. Do this for all buckets. The hole will be for the bulkhead fitting. Make sure this is close to the edge of the bucket, so that the system will still be stable if you stick it on a flat surface, such as the edge of a patio table. Be very cautious that the holes are not too big- otherwise your system may leak.

    a. Use a drill, with the appropriate sized bit. This will help you get the round shape for the bulkhead fitting, while also keeping the edge smooth. A smooth edge is important to ensure the fitting will line up and create a tight seal.

    b. You should have an O-ring or rubber ring on the inside of the bucket to create a non-leaking seal. Some fittings may have this on the other side, right under the nut.

2. You are going to put the bulkhead fittings into the hole you have created. The fitting should be placed inside the bucket, with the longer end going through the hole to the outside. The nut will go on the outside to hold the bulkhead in place. The longest portion of the fitting will have a tub fit over it, which is why the long side will go through the bottom of the bucket to the outside, and then have the nut fit over it to keep it in place. Use a wrench to tighten the nut to prevent water from leaking.

    a. An extra step can be to use a sealant, such as caulking around the bulkhead fitting and nut. Caulking on the outside of the fitting will not contaminate the nutrient solution, but it will prevent leaks.

    b. Wait to attach the tubing to the nut.

3. You need to protect the buckets from heat and light to prevent damage to the roots and discourage the growth of algae and mold. Begin by putting electrical tape all around the bulkhead fitting- you do not want any paint to get on it! This is necessary even if you have caulked around the fitting. Make sure to cover the entire fitting, not just around the nut, since you will use spray paint. If you did caulk around the fitting wait until it is dry, it usually takes 8 hours.

4. Turn the bucket upside down on a tarp or plastic. Start spray painting several coats of black paint. You will want to do this until you cannot see any light coming through the bucket. You also need to wait for each coat of black paint to dry, before you begin the next layer. Spray paint will dry quickly; especially, in the sun. Touch the paint to check if it is dry. If it feels tacky, wait a few more minutes before spraying the next layer.

5. After the black paint is completely dry, spray a few layers of white paint over the top. Again, wait for each layer of paint to dry, before spraying a new layer. Since black attracts heat, using white paint will help stop heat from damaging the roots.

6. While you are doing this, you should also paint the tote you are using for the reservoir. Start with a black coat and wait until it is completely dry and light proof, before adding the white layer.

7. Now that the bucket is prepared, it is time to install the filter. You will need to remove the filter part from the furnace filter. This needs to be placed across the area where the thread nuts are located. Its purpose is to keep the growing material out of the tubing, while still allowing the excess nutrient solution to

drip down. Consider a vegetable container like a lettuce keeper for your fridge. There is a plastic insert in true produce containers to ensure the product is kept from sitting in water that may be dripping off the clean vegetables. The filter will separate the rocks and growing material from the bulkhead fittings and drainage tubing.

8. You are going to lay down your rocks and your growing medium. First, lay a couple inches of rocks at the bottom of the bucket. These will weigh down the filter, as well as keep the bucket bottom-heavy so that it is less likely to tip over, if you will keep your system outside in the wind.

9. Fill the bucket with the growing medium (fill until it is a few inches from the top of the bucket). This is the perlite, clay balls or coconut coir. The growing medium is what will help keep the roots in place and allow the plant to grow in an upwards position, rather than falling out of the buckets.

10. Now, it is time to make the watering lines. Begin by taking tubing and making an "O". Fasten this to either end of a T-connector. Both ends of the tubing will go into the T connector to create a complete circle. The T connector will be parallel with the tubing, while the short part of the connector is still available for the incoming water line.

11. Heat up the end of a paper clip and use it to make small holes in the circle tubing. Place this around your bucket. Do this for each of the 4 buckets. The holes are to allow the water nutrient solution to come out of the tubing and sink into the roots of your plants.

12. Run piping from the T-connector to your reservoir. The tube will be connected to a pump, which pumps the nutrient solution and water through the piping and into the growing medium, where the plant will absorb it.

    a. The extra solution will be filtered to remove any plant matter or growing material and then drip down into a reservoir to be used again.

    b. Make sure there is only one main line going into the pump. The water pump will have an outgoing connector that your tubing will fit over. There is no need for a T-connector at the water pump.

13. Run a tube from the bulkhead fittings into the reservoir. The reservoir needs to be 6 inches from the bottom of your buckets, thus you need to measure the tube accordingly.

14. Setting up the reservoir is also needed. Painting it and getting the tubes the right length to run from the pump to the T-connector and from the bulkhead fittings to the reservoir is just a part of the reservoir system. The filter in the bottom of the buckets is meant to catch most of the medium, so it will not go through the tubing; however, you may elect to add an additional filter system in the reservoir. You can divide your reservoir into two parts, where the nutrient water is kept separate from the drainage water, until it passes through a filter to clean it. You also need to have a lid for the reservoir, but access to it, so you can check the pH of the water.

15. Connect a digital timer to the pump.

16. If you are growing outside, you will also want to take the necessary precautions to protect your timer and electrical cords from getting wet. The first thing to do is buy all outdoor equipment, including an outdoor timer such as those made for sprinkler systems. They are designed to get wet versus indoor systems. Also, you may need lights to protect your plants from cooler temperatures depending on where you live.

Green houses and indoor plant rooms may also need grow lights or plant lights to ensure they are receiving the proper sunlight and warmth. If you live in a place with four seasons or long winters, it will be necessary to have an indoor space for most fruits and vegetables.

Stabilizing your System

Since sitting the buckets on the ground is not an option, you will need some sort of device to keep the buckets and reservoir 6 inches apart. A specially designed table will be best and inexpensive.

1. Measure 8 2x4s to stand 36 inches.

2. Measure 2 2x4s to be the width of your bucket. Measure the bucket width from underneath the lip. Most buckets have a lip or three rings that extend out from the smooth surface of the bucket. You can use this lip to sit on the edge of the 2x4, which is why you want the distance to be tight.

3. Measure 2 2x4s to be the length of four buckets lined up in a row.

The height of the 2x4s was chosen to accommodate the bucket height, as well as a more comfortable height for picking vegetables and fruits from your plants. If necessary, you can increase this height or lower it, but make certain you have at least 6 inches from the reservoir or more for drainage. If you build the structure high enough the drainage can sit under the middle buckets, but still provide access to test the water.

Additionally, create a support 2x4 for the back of the structure. The support 2x4 should run from the bottom of one leg to the top of the diagonal leg, meaning it needs to run diagonal to the length of the longest 2x4. You can also create a brace between each of the 8 supporting legs, which would be measured the same size as the width of the structure.

Chapter 5: Fruits - A Growing Cheat Sheet

For many of us who are looking to get into hydroponic gardening, our first thought might be which sorts of fruits and vegetables can be grown here, and what sorts of factors do you need to take into consideration when it comes to growing these types of gardens. You know how to build the garden, but there are a few maintenance tips that will ensure you have the best hydroponic garden, and these are based off the various fruits, vegetables, and herbs that are able to be grown there easily. This chapter will go into hydroponic gardening tips for these various fruits and vegetables that you can plant in your hydroponic garden.

Popular Fruits

You are starting your garden because you want healthy food, readily available, and a sustainable life. Some fruits do better in hydroponic gardens than others, but this does not mean you can't grow any fruit you desire. You just need to know the specifics of certain fruits to avoid common growing mistakes. There are also fruits that do very well in hydroponic setups like tomatoes, cantaloupe and watermelon. Before you grow any fruit the biggest thing you need to watch out for are the growing conditions.

Melons

Watermelons, for example, are heat and water loving plants. Watermelons are vining plants, with heavy fruits, so why they do well in hydroponic systems, you still need to provide a certain level of care and attention; particularly, regarding nutrient solution, lighting and weight support. Watermelons are best grown in greenhouses or outside. If you want more than two or three plants, you will need to choose an ebb-and-flow system. If you grow one or two plants, a floating hydroponic system can be a good option. The growing medium should have support to keep the roots in place and help the vines grow. Heavier pea gravel, clay pellets, or silica stones are best. You can also mix in sand for stability. Once the fruit starts to grow, you will want it to have somewhere it can rest, whether it is on the ground, a table, or in a clear container.

Similar in nature are cantaloupes, thus the same care, attention, and even temperature requirements. These have a skin that is great for the ebb and flow system due to the hard surface. You should make sure that these are supported as well by nets or another type of support.

Most melons, including the two mentioned above, grow well in temperatures of 72 to 90 degrees Fahrenheit, but can go as low as 61 or as high as 93 degrees Fahrenheit. If you grow melons from seeds, germination is best at 82 to 86 degrees Fahrenheit. You germinate the seeds and then place the young plants in the hydroponics system within two weeks. You want to supply a standard fruiting and vegetative nutrient formula to your plants; however, for melons it should be high in potassium during the fruiting periods. As soon as fruits begin to grow, increase the potassium level. You also want to maintain a large, healthy leaf area to ensure proper fruiting. You need to limit your fruit to 3 or 4 per plant to keep the flavor.

Melons grow well in a pH of 6.5 to 6.8. It is a smaller range, thus require a good amount of control.

Fruit Trees

Fruit trees can also be grown in a hydroponic manner in some cases. Banana trees, for example, can be grown in this manner, and if you're looking to get a dwarf citrus tree, it will feel right at home provided you give them the right conditions. You will want to make sure they get enough light. That's the major factor with many of these fruit trees, because if they're not grown with the correct light, it will be problematic.

Most of the dwarf citrus trees commonly grown in hydroponic systems are lemon, orange, and mandarin. Like the melons, a lot of light and warm weather are necessary to keep these plants growing. Unless, you have an indoor greenhouse, you will want to have LED growing lamps to provide proper lighting, at the very least you should have halide or high pressure sodium lamps. Starting citrus trees from seedlings will take 3 to 5 years for it to start bearing fruit. You are better off getting a plant that is already growing, but this can also provide some difficult situations. For example, you would need to find a hydroponic grower to buy your citrus trees from to avoid issues with replanting a soil based tree. It is recommended that you use a Hoagland solution, one specifically designed for fruit trees. Iron and manganese are two nutrients fruit trees need and rarely get from the soil, which is why the Hoagland solution works best.

For the temperature, as you know most citrus trees are tropical plants. They like warm zones such as Florida, Georgia, Hawaii, and the Caribbean. While citrus trees will not die at temperatures of 32 degrees Fahrenheit, you are going to tempt fate. It is better to grow these plants in temperatures of 70 to 90 degrees Fahrenheit. For the pH you want it between 5.5 and 6.5.

Pineapple bushes can fit into tropical plants, with regards to most of the growing conditions mentioned; however, the pH level should be 5 to 5.5, versus slightly more neutral. With pineapples, drip systems work great because you can place the top of a pineapple into the medium and let water drip down, without getting the pineapple top too wet. With pineapples, you can twist the top off an existing fruit, cut away the flesh until you see little red spots, and then plant the top in your garden. It will root, start to grow, and in two years bear fruit. Pineapple is a little slower than most tropical plants, since it does take 2 full years for it to start producing a new fruit. You can get at least two fruits on the same bush. The old stalk will die, but a new stalk will form, with new leaf growth. As long as the roots remain healthy, you can continue to get fruit from the plant.

Banana trees and other dwarf plants do well in NFT grow systems. Banana trees will not like temperatures below 67 degrees Fahrenheit, so they are perfect to grow alongside citrus trees. Bananas are also heavy feeders, so you will need to add grow medium to your hydroponic system on a weekly basis, although at high growth times you can use 1/3 of the growth medium and all other times use the full strength solution. Your bananas also need 12 hours of sunlight. Like the citrus trees, the pH level can be 5.5 to 6.5.

Berries

There are different types of berries that can be grown hydroponically, if you know what you are doing. You also have to understand that berries grow very differently, such as strawberries, which have a vining system versus a bush like blueberries.

Strawberries are one of the easiest fruits to grow in an outdoor soil garden, but they can also be grown hydroponically. Humidity for certain strawberry plants is not a bad thing, such as the strawberries grown in places like North Carolina. However, when it comes to hydroponic gardening, you do need to limit the humidity and water to avoid root rot. An NFT system is best for strawberries since you have more control over the system and can reduce the humidity to prevent root rot.

If you start off with strawberry seeds it will take 2 to 3 years before you can pull the fruit. If you want strawberries sooner, simply start with a plant that is already mature or a plug, which is a rooted runner that will root into your medium and start to bear fruit earlier. With most strawberries, when a plant is producing runners it is not going to bear fruit. Every other year runners are formed and thus every other year, opposite the runners, nice plump strawberries will appear. Also consider purchasing June bearing strawberries.

For strawberries the pH level is optimal at 5.5 to 6. Growing temperatures should be 65 to 72 degrees Fahrenheit, with a 14- hour light cycle.

Blueberries grow on bushes, much like blackberries and raspberries. You also need to realize that these plants take a long time to grow and mature, which means the fruit is usually not provided until the second year. However, the bush will keep producing fruit, so there is a cost effectiveness to growing blueberries at home. You will not need to replant the blueberry bush either, which you would have to do if you grew it in a pot with soil. Like strawberries the blueberry bush does best in the NFT system. There is one drawback to having a small NFT system, with multiple types of fruits and vegetables. Blueberries grow at a lower pH than most. They thrive in 4.5 to 5.8 pH, with a temperature between 72 and 76 degrees Fahrenheit. Blueberries also require 12 to 16 hours of daylight. The humidity range should be 65 to 75 percent.

You can follow the guidelines for blueberries for most other berry bushes, like loganberries. The key is to maintain the system.

Grapes

Technically, you could call grapes, fruit trees; however, they deserve their own section because many have found it more difficult to grow grapes hydroponically. Grapes need a well-supported system with the proper nutrient flow, without letting the plant tip over due to the weight of the grape bunches. The roots of grapes can also rot with relative ease. A drip system will work with grapes. It will also allow you to use a trellis so the plant can vine upwards. Grapes need full sun and the pH should be slightly acidic to neutral, meaning 6.5 to 7.

Tomatoes

Tomatoes are another amazing fruit to grow in your garden as well, because even if you don't' like to eat them raw, they can be used as a sauce or paste for many dishes. You should plant these in a soilless planting mix with a trellis for the best results. They are vine plants, so do watch how they grow. You should use a drip system if you can as well, because these yield great results.

Tomatoes were one of the first plants to be grown hydroponically and with such astounding success that it has become almost second nature to grow them in a drip system versus in soil conditions. Tomato plants are one that can become diseased very easily in the wrong conditions; particularly, with improper soil. This is why they thrive in hydroponic systems where you maintain the nutrient solution, pH and prevent pests from getting to the plants. Tomatoes require a pH level of 5.5 to 6.5, which fits in with most of the other fruit plants you might decide to grow. For tomatoes using rock wool, lava rock, or coco peat is usually best for the planting medium.

It has been suggested to water new plantings for 15 or 30 minutes, four times a day. Tomatoes like water, but they can wilt in too much sun, thus the need for frequent watering. Once the plants start to bloom and fruit, it is best to increase the water. Tomatoes need plenty of nutrients to keep healthy. Also, if using artificial light, provide 16 to 18 hours of light. A plant will grow more slowly with only 8 hours of sun. Make sure to stake your tomato plant. The heavy fruit will cause it to pull down and it might stop growing properly. Tomato plants also grow best in temperatures of 65 to 75 degrees Fahrenheit.

There are certainly plenty of other fruits out there that you might wish to grow. This is a highlight of the most popular types of fruits that people want to grow. If there is a type of fruit not mentioned or that does not fit into the category, you will need to conduct more research before planting anything.

Chapter 6: Vegetables - A Growing Cheat Sheet

Vegetables in general are the staple of most hydroponic gardens, since they can be grown year-round and don't take that much room. However, they do have a couple of general growing tips.

General Growing Tips

For many vegetables, you should space them about a foot apart to prevent fighting of the root systems over water and other such nutrients that they need. They do take up a whole lot less space, and you should make sure that they get the right light and warmth. Also make sure that you control the size of these plants as well, because they can get out of hand when it comes to growing too large.

Artichokes, beets, cabbages, celery, radishes, parsnips, leeks, broccoli, carrots, onion, eggplant, Brussel sprouts, potatoes, cauliflower and squash are the best vegetables to grow in a hydroponic garden. Now, these will thrive, but some grow better than others, so it's important to know that they all don't grow equally in terms of simplicity.

Lettuce and Leafy Vegetables

In terms of types of veggies to grow, one of the best is actually lettuce. Lettuce and leafy vegetables are great for any salad or sandwich, so it will be considered a staple in the kitchen. However, they are pretty easy to take care of, and they grow super-fast in hydroponic gardens. The best way to grow these is with a nutrient film technique system (NFT). Using water and mineral salts for nutrients plus gravel for the medium is a good way to get healthy, continual lettuce. You can also use sand, sawdust, shavings, and vermiculite for the medium. Lettuce requires 15 to 18 hours of light per day. For the pH level make sure it stays within 6 to 6.5.

Root Vegetables

The vegetables in this section are root vegetables, meaning you eat the roots versus the part that will grow out of the earth. In fact, most of the vegetables can be considered root based like carrots and potatoes. Still, there are things like lettuce, which can grow underground or grow up from the root.

Radishes are a great vegetable as well, because the flavor is great in them, whether they're raw, grilled, pickled, or even snappy, and they work well with other vegetables. These are one of the easiest to grow, and if you use a direct water culture system, you will get the best results possible. For radishes, experts suggest perlite, growstones, clay pellets, rice husks, coconut peat, gravel, sand, or wood fiber as a growing medium. You want a porous material, so the root has a place to expand and grow, providing you with a healthy 1-inch size radishes. Radishes grow best at a pH level of 6 to 7. Radishes have a growth temperature of 50 to 65 degrees Fahrenheit, where they need 8 to 10 hours of sun.

Potatoes can be grown hydroponically; however, it takes a real expert to make it happen. For a beginner, you are better off to start with easier root vegetables. In saying that it is difficult, you can still make it happen, as long as you pay special attention to your potatoes. They will need a medium that they can root in, which means perlite, clay pellets, coconut coir or sand. This gives the roots a chance to expand, as well as to actually begin growing in the first place. The pH level is 5.8 to 6.2, which is a very narrow window compared to many of the other plants we have discussed. Temperatures are right there with cucumbers at 65 to 75 degrees Fahrenheit. Potatoes need 10 to 12 hours of sunlight a day, but can survive with 6 hours. The one thing that can truly hinder your potato success is root rot. In excessive humidity, potatoes will rot very quickly, which means they may not develop beyond a small tuber and certainly nothing delicious. Ideally, have a drip system using coco-coir or a soilless potting soil system to grow potatoes.

Carrots, like potatoes can be a real challenge. You need good air flow for carrots because they need to root. In soil, you can squeeze a carrot too much, so it has stunted growth. With hydroponics, the trouble is getting it to root in the first place. You will want a drip system with coconut coir, sand, perlite, or clay pellets. The great thing about carrots is they grow in a variety of temperatures from 50 to 85 degrees Fahrenheit. You do need to provide 12 to 16 hours of daylight for your carrots. The harvest is about 12 months, which is difficult for outdoor gardens that will start to see frost and cooler temperatures; however, you can always make sure to plant these roots inside.

Onions are another root vegetable. They will grow in the ground and need to be dug up when the time is right. For a hydroponic system, you might consider a drip setup. You will want to use Rockwool or composite plugs. Onions do well in 65 to 70 degree Fahrenheit temperatures. They also take 80 to 90 days before you can harvest them. Onions are prone to issues with nitrogen, so you want to monitor the pH often. For onions, the pH should be 6.5 to 7. Onions also require approximately 12 hours of sunlight each day.

Garlic, even when growing can have a fairly bad stench. It is a plant better grown outside, but it can certainly be done in a hydroponic system. You will want to bury a clove in coconut coir to get the best results. The clove will root and in 45 to 60 days, you will be able to pick the garlic out of the ground. A healthy green stalk, with four to five leaves will appear above ground, then as the garlic gets closer to harvest it the stalk and leaves will die. Garlic is one plant that has an ideal growing condition of 35 to 50 degrees Fahrenheit, with 40 degrees being optimal. This is why you can grow it outside, even in cooler places, at least during the spring and fall. Garlic will need 10 to 12 hours of light. You should also supply a pH level of 6 to 6.5. It is a small range, but possible when you follow proper guidelines. Garlic is also a plant that is unique because it is less likely to be affected by pests and diseases, in fact, it is more of a natural pest repellent than anything. The only trouble is white rot, which can also attack onions.

Broccoli

A nice green vegetable, broccoli can be grown in a hydroponic system. The pH level should be 6 to 6.8. You also want the temperature around 50 to 60 degrees Fahrenheit. This is one of those plants that might not fit in your greenhouse or other gardening area, because it has a lower temperature rating; although you can stretch it to 70 degrees Fahrenheit with proper watering, once the plant starts to break through the surface of whatever medium you have chosen. Perlite, gravel or clay pebbles are good mediums. Broccoli grows best in 10 to 12 hours of daylight. The hydroponic system should be a drip system with a proper drain. Broccoli tends to suffer root rot, when there is too much water. The timer for your system should be once a day, perhaps twice depending on how much water comes through each time. You definitely need to set it up, test the medium, and adjust the controls. For this reason, and the others stated, you may want to avoid broccoli unless you have the space for it to be on its own system.

Celery

Celery is a great one for those looking to get on a diet. The reason for this, is because celery is a negative calorie, which means that you will be burning calories just eating it. Plus, the flavor and texture of it will make a delectable food for just about anyone. Ideally, you should invest in an ebb and flow system for these vegetables, and you should make sure that the water isn't too much for them, since their roots are very shallow and if you're not careful, they are prone to drowning.

When it comes to the conditions for celery growth, you will need a constant 70 degrees Fahrenheit for your plants. You will also want to ensure direct sunlight for 12 to 16 hours a day. It is best to use mesh netting and lay perlite on top of it to help the plant root. If you go from seeds instead of plants, you need 5 celery seeds every 2 inches. It will take 5 weeks for celery to sprout from the ground. It should be harvested 4 months after planting the seeds for optimal taste.

Vining Vegetable

Cucumbers can be turned into some many great, including many different salads and sandwiches. They are also very simple to grow in many cases. If you use a drip irrigation system, you will get the best results possible. You want to target a pH level of 5.5 to 6. It also needs to be mentioned that cucumbers and tomatoes tend to compete for root area and they both vine, so you do not want your cucumbers and tomatoes in the same planter or next to each other. Cucumbers also need moderate humidity, with temperatures ranging from 65 degrees to 80 degrees Fahrenheit. Cucumbers are also less friendly in the sun than tomatoes, so provide only 8 to 12 hours of sunlight.

Peppers

Peppers are by far one of the easiest plants to grow, if you start off with a mature plant. Starting from seeds may encounter a few problems, simply because it takes more time. From the time you see a stalk start growing for a pepper it takes 60 to 70 days for it to be ready to harvest. You will need to use a Rockwool or perlite medium for your plant. You also want to ensure it gets 10 to 12 hours of sun a day. The temperature should be at least 70 degrees Fahrenheit, but it is better to be 73 to 80. The pH level can be as low as 5.5 up to neutral.

You can add sodium hydroxide or potassium hydroxide to water to increase the pH when it is low. One other thing should be mentioned with regards to pepper plants—the color of the pepper is determined by when you pick it. A green pepper will begin to grow; however, as you leave the pepper on the plant it will turn different shades and become red, yellow or orange depending on when you decide to pick it. A lot of times the green pepper is cheaper in stores because it is picked right away and growers can move along in the growing process, whereas, if they wait there is more time needed for vegetable care.

As vegetables go, there are plenty, which have not been mentioned. Cauliflower, kale, and mushrooms are just three other vegetables that you might consider growing in your garden. When you do look for other plants, whether it is a variety of legumes or various types of lettuce, remember that each plant has its own growing conditions. Highlights for popular vegetables have been mentioned here to help you get your garden started. You always want to read up on each individual plant, check the harvesting time, and remember to plan your garden around the growing conditions required.

Chapter 7: Herbs – A Growing Cheat Sheet

Herbs are a very rewarding type of plant to grow. If you want something that yields a result fast, require less care, and can be used in just about every dish you want, then these are for you. You can have a small system to grow these, and they give you a great crop.

If you want to start with a hydroponic garden, you should try out some herbs first. You can grow arugula, chives, lemon balm, oregano, spear, peppermint, thyme, basil, coriander, Mache, rosemary, sage, dill, chervil, marjoram, sorrel, and tarragon easily within a hydroponic garden. You can see from that list that these herbs are used in a variety of foods, so you definitely will get some great results with these.

A drip system or one of the inexpensive $30 hydroponic systems sold as herb gardens will work great. You get everything you could want to grow your plants all in one kit. Of course, you do have to use the herbs quickly as they grow very fast. A 12 by 24-inch box is really all you need for dozens of herbs.

Benefits of Growing Herbs

There are several reasons that you want to grow herbs above all other vegetables and fruits. It is the medicinal properties, herbs can provide. Yes, vegetables and fruits contain antioxidants, minerals, and nutrients your body needs; however, herbs can also be used for several topical applications, as well as skin care products. With your herb garden you can create sleep remedies, like soothing lavender or chamomile. Oregano is known to help with colds, so it is a great herb for a tea mixture, as well as to use in various recipes. Sometimes, a small plant that grows like a weed is simply the best way to sustain life. There are a few growing tips to note though.

General Growing Tips

Using an ebb and flow system is often best for various herbs. You can also use plastic pots, with perlite as the growing medium. You want to water your herbs every 5 to 6 hours, for 15 minutes to get good root saturation. The pH level of most herbs is 5.5 to 6. When it comes to nutrients most herbs have specifics like arugula requires 0.4 ppm more copper than other herbs and basil requires 80 ppm more magnesium. PPM stands for parts per million. Herbs also tend to grow better under soft grow lights, with a short 10-hour plan versus a longer light plan. It has been suggested that you will want to use a 400-watt metal halide light or 1000-watt light for an area of 6 feet.

Herbs also need more air circulation than some of the vegetables and fruits you might grow. It is best to keep a hydroponic ventilation system and carbon dioxide enrichment system attached to your herb system. The air temperature needs to be 70 to 75 degrees Fahrenheit. The humidity should remain between 40 and 60 percent.

When it comes to harvesting your herbs, you can let the plants continue to grow or you can remove the herbs all at once and save them, which you will learn about later.

Chives

Chives is one herb that is great for just about any dish you want to garnish. If you want something easy to grow and maintain, this is it. You should use an ebb and flow system or a drip system for the best results. Chives are also a plant that you may use more often than some of the other herbs in this chapter.

Oregano

Oregano is another one that goes with just about everything. You should make sure that with this one you have an ebb and flow or even a drip system for it to work best. For those starting out, this is a great one to start off with, because oregano is an herb that's even part of the hydroponic home kit that you see, meaning it's so easy to grow that anyone can do it, and if you want something simple, fun, and yields great results, check this one out.

Basil

For basil, you should have an NFT or a drip system to get the best results. It does grow very quickly, and the great part is that it doesn't take up a ton of room. If you have a spot in your garden that is tiny and needs a special plant, then this is a great one to consider. Basil has medicinal properties. It contains anti-bacterial properties, so eating it is great, but you can also use it as an oil. For an oil, you would take fresh leaves, add a little water, and start heating it. As you create the infusion, add in a little coconut oil and you will get a nice green tinged oil to rub on your cuts.

Anise

An ideal pH level is 6, but why do you want to know this? It is because anise is just one of the many herb plants that you can grow for its medicinal benefits. It provides the licorice taste to many foods, include baked and stewed fruits. It can be used to flavor tea or help make cough drops taste better. It is also a digestive helper, so a little anise after you eat too much or when you have an upset stomach will definitely make you feel better.

Sage

This is good for those who like to have a bit more of a peppery flavor to it. It's an essential herb for those who love to cook with herbs, and with a hydroponic garden, it's actually easy to grow. NFT is the best system for this one, but unlike the others, it can be grown with a different system if you want to grow it near other herbs that have a different system.

Rosemary

Rosemary is one that is great for meals to use, and it is an essential herb to help you make bread with. For anyone who wants to grow rosemary, it's important to note the roots of it are fibrous, so you should make sure to incorporate either a drip system or a soilless potting mix in order to get the best results from this.

Mint

Mint is one of the few herbs that will do better between 6.5 and 7 pH. You definitely want this gem in your hydroponic herb garden though because it is a digestive and anti-bloating agent. Ladies, if you have issues with your menstrual cycle, this is the herb to start adding to your tea or simply to an infused water concoction. Mint helps with cramps, bloating, and other digestive problems that can be worse at this time of the month.

Saving Herbs

Since herbs grow quickly, you can have several batches of herbs and not enough meals to put them into. This is going to happen if you decide to grow more than a dozen herbs in your garden because you want each one for a specific purpose or taste. The point being—you need a way to save the herbs, so you can use them rather than throw them away. Another option is to give your friends and family some herbs each time you have a good batch ready.

To save herbs, you will need to pluck the plants, leave the roots, but take the part of the plant you use for cooking. The roots will produce more herbs. Once you have harvested the herbs lay them out to dry for a few hours in the sun. The herbs will become dry and then you can use your mortar and pestle to chop them up, put them in a mason jar, and store in a cool, dry area, with little sun.

You can also create herbal tisanes from these dried leaves, infuse them in water for 10 to 15 minutes and drink it as an herbal remedy, much like tea. These are just a few of the additional uses and ways you can save the herbs you are growing in case you are unable to use them all before they need to be harvested.

Overall, herbs are a great system to grow it, and you should start with these if you're just starting out. They are so small that you can grow these on a window sill or even a kitchen top if you so desire, and you will get fresh and savory ingredients from this. If you're looking for something tasty to have, then growing these is the best for you.

All of these plants have various different systems that you can grow them in. This chapter showed you some of the best plants to grow, and some growing habits to keep in mind. Once you start growing them as well, you can work with these and change them up to best fit you, but these are what you should start with, and what works best in a hydroponic garden.

Chapter 8: Planning Your Garden

You have learned a great deal about fruits, herbs, and vegetables you can grow. It is time to focus a little on the planning it takes to get your garden set up. If you are like most people, you will have limited space, where you can put your hydroponic system. Plenty has to go into the location you will put your plants, as well as how many plants you can have.

Zones

In agriculture there are zones, such as zone 1 and zone 7. These zones are based on climate. When you start your hydroponic garden you will want to study various plants like those listed in previous chapters and determine which zone they grow in. Tropical plants are considered zone 1, whereas hemlock plants are considered zone 6 or 7 because they can grow in colder areas. Of course, hemlock is a tree and not a food bearing plant, but the point is, you need to look at the types of plants you want to have and figure out which zone they grow best in.

Indoor versus Outdoor Hydroponic Systems

Later you are going to learn about pests and how to avoid using pesticides. One reason to have an outdoor garden is to avoid pesticides by using natural pesticides i.e. other bugs that eat the ones harming your plant. With inside gardens, you do not want to introduce more bugs into the garden.

However, there is more to an indoor versus outdoor garden question than just pests. It goes back to the zone you live in versus the zone the plants are from. What if you wanted to grow pineapple in Alaska? Sure, the sunlight is perfect, but temperatures rarely become warm enough for a long enough period of time. Plus, it takes years for a pineapple plant to grow and produce fruit, which means during the cold, no sun months the plant would die. So, a large part of whether you will grow your garden inside or outside is based on the plants you intend on putting in the garden.

With an indoor garden you also have more environmental control. You get to set the temperature, add lighting if the daylight is not enough, and prevent rainwater from watering your plants in addition to your hydroponic system. What would happen if rain is continually accessing your plant? It would be getting water, but the nutrient levels would become less potent because the solution would be diluted by extra water. You may also end up overwatering your plants.

Now, you may have a problem with space in your home. If you live in an apartment growing indoors means restricted areas for growing plants. You might have to choose multiple corners or lose the use of one entire room. If you do want to grow a hydroponic garden indoors, you may also have to consider if one room gets better sunlight for longer periods of the day.

For those that own a home with property, there is a solution to going entirely outdoors with your garden. You can erect a greenhouse, there are some small, inexpensive options, as well as the more expensive structures, but at least you could have something over your plants to protect them against the outdoor elements, while also maintaining control over temperature.

Space and Design

Once you have planned where you can put your hydroponic system, you will need to determine how to design the space you have. There are limitations to the amount of plants you can put into one bucket or how many types of plants you can put into one bucket. Some plants have more roots and others less, but there are also competing plants, which can kill each other or at least limit the growth of one.

You may like the idea of putting various plants together for the pop of color you get when the fruit and vegetables start to grow, but again, you must be spatially aware of the limitations of combining plants.

It is far better to consider using one bucket, tray, or planter per plant. If space is limited, at least design with the limitations in mind to get as many plants in one area as possible. Herbs are great for getting multiple types all in one little area.

You also have to consider that some plants vine, which means they will grow tall or spread out side ways to produce more fruits and veggies. Strawberries, cucumbers, and tomatoes are at least three plants that you have to provide enough space for, plus ensure that there is room to expand. You can keep some of these plants relatively small, with regards to leaves and by pruning non-essential stems and leaves way, but you still need to ensure the fruit has a proper cover from sunlight.

Given that you can design your own hydroponic system with buckets and bins, you may also want to consider if you would be better off designing your own system and buying the pieces to construct it. By designing your own, you get to determine the space it takes up, not only width, but length. You can also use corners more efficiently. For example, you could have a planter that is 6 inches by 4 feet. It is low profile and can run along a window. You can also cut it to fit in a corner and continue around that corner to another area.

If you are less inclined to design or do not feel comfortable doing so, then it is enough to plan out the various plants, check the zone it grows in, and start buying the necessary supplies for the controlled environment you need.

Temperature and Humidity

You will learn that most plants can coexist due to high and low ends of the temperature and humidity spectrum. Some plants do better at 65 degrees Fahrenheit, but can live in temperatures 5 degrees hotter. Other plants can live in temperatures of 70 and up, but nothing lower. There is also a specific humidity range to keep most plants too, which you will learn later. For now, you just need to keep these different requirements in mind and understand that you can combine plants as long as you use the highs of some plant conditions and the lows of other plant requirements.

Lighting

You will see a lot of sections about lighting. This one is specific to planning, so it won't detail the types of lights or using daylight. It is just necessary to remind you that, certain plants need direct sunlight and others do not. You want to plan your hydroponic garden around the lights and shadows that naturally occur in your greenhouse or gardening room. If growing plants outside, then you will need some systems that are more in a shaded area, with some sunlight versus direct sunlight. It goes back to putting some plants in the same system versus ensuring they are never in the same system. You don't want direct sunlight plants in with non-direct sunlight plants, since some will not get proper shade or perhaps proper lighting depending on how you place the system.

With these planning tips, you have an idea of the structure or at least how to start thinking about the structure of your garden. It is always best to get a few pieces of paper, so you can write out your plant list and draw out the plan for where these plants will go. When you have a picture of how you want the plants to go, as well as one to remind you of what plants can be in the same system, you will have a better setup overall. It is also something you can refer to if you have questions about what you intended once you buy the plants.

Chapter 9: Water Maintenance, Garden Expansion, and More: Tips from the Experts on Hydroponics

Now that you know a bit more about how to plant your garden, it's time to go over some tips. There are a few things of note when it comes to a hydroponic garden, and these are important to learn. Taking care of your garden is what you need to do, and this chapter will give you the best tips on how to get the most out of your hydroponic garden so it will be successful.

Water Maintenance

Maintaining water is one of the key factors in a hydroponic garden. You might be starting off, and giving your plants the right water, but they're not growing. However, there are a few tips that can help you with this.

If the medium is still wet, don't water. Sometimes, these hydroponic gardens take a bit more time in terms of growth. The plants might not grow as fast as you believe they should because the roots may not be absorbing the water right away. It does not mean you should stop watering or taking care of the plants. Typically, you should make sure that it is getting the right nutrients, and you should make sure that it's not getting overwatered. It is all about the combination of water and nutrients.

Ensure that the humidity is taken care of at all times. Different plants need different humidity levels, so it's important to note that some plants will need more and others will need less. Do take time to research your plants so that you're not giving them the wrong care.

If you're using chlorinated tap water in a reservoir, you should fill the reservoir or mixing bin and let the water sit for a day to help get rid of the chlorine. You should try to get rid of as much of it as possible, because the chlorine doesn't help with plant growth. It is in fact best if you avoid using tap water at all. Tap water has its own mixture of chemicals and purifications to make it safe for us to drink, but that also means it can contain too much of something a plant needs or something that can kill a plant altogether.

You should also look into getting a timer for the water pump. Usually, an all-purpose timer is one of the best for this. You should get a 15-amp timer because they last longer and it is barely a dollar more for the better timer. Also, purchasing a dial versus a digital timer is better, since the digital timer needs electricity to work. You should look for the settings that you need, and you should look to see if there is a 15-minute setting on there to help you. For the best water maintenance, you need a timer attached to the water pump. In this way you are sure your plants are getting watered at appropriate intervals, and never without water when it needs it.

Temperature also determined the amount you will need to water your plants. Hot, humid days will require more watering than cooler days. Of course, certain plants handle hot temperatures better than others, thus the finger test into the medium, which allows you to check if the medium is still wet or if more watering is needed. The one thing you do not want to do is let the roots become dry.

Make certain when considering water and temperature that you have like plants in your hydroponic system. In other words, do not put a pineapple and tomato plant on the same hydroponic watering timer because tomatoes need more water than a pineapple plant. Set your garden up so that plants that need to be watered each day, once a week, or a few times a week are on the appropriate cycle. It is a low maintenance way to ensure your plants are watered, getting proper nutrients, and growing faster than if you were using soil.

Garden Expansion

When it comes to expanding your garden, there are a few things that you should know, because they are definitely important to keep in mind before you start to grow in a hydroponic garden.

Lighting

If you are growing a hydroponic garden in a place that has a somewhat outdoor setting such as a sun room, you need to ensure that the area is getting light. When you are expanding, do consider the light factors that are necessary for this. Yes, grow lights do work in many cases, and they can be helpful, but you should also have natural light as well to keep the plants thriving. You should work to have at least all of the plants near two corners of the wall, and have windows that will allow the plant to absorb the light. Ideally, try to get as many of them near the window as possible, if not grown in a greenhouse. If necessary, add more lights to ensure the proper amount of sunlight; especially, if you notice your plants are struggling to get proper lighting from windows.

Fixtures

There are various fixtures. Some of the pots are good for garden expansion. You should make sure that you get a trellis or a potting system that has multiple planters so that you can grow more. Ideally, you want to consider all sorts of planter sizes, so that some will fit into small areas and others can fit in areas with more space.

Finally, you should make sure that the plants are given enough space. It happens frequently that when you're expanding, you think you can just put more in the location and expect it to be fine. In reality, that's not going to work, and you will end up creating more problems in your garden than you expected. What you should do instead, is trying to figure out new places that work for the plant, and also keep in mind the size of it.

You might think you have plenty of space in one planter, until you realize that the roots of one single plant have spread out. For example, carrots need to be spaced 6 to 12 inches apart and have plenty of room to grow down. If you have too many seeds in one hole, without trimming back the amount of new growth to one carrot top, there is not enough room for a full size carrot.

Remember that vegetables need approximately a foot of room for them to grow so that the roots don't crowd, but in contrast, herbs don't need a ton of growing space, which makes it work for many. You should research what plants will work for which spaces, and what works for you.

When it comes to space and planting various fruits and vegetables, there are other things to consider, such as plant compatibility. Have you ever planted vegetables in the same large box planter and had one thrive while the other died, yet the year before you could grow the one that died just fine? It comes down to compatibility. There are certain competing plants that cannot grow together in the same space. If you use the drip bucket system as outlined in previous chapters, you would want to have one bucket for each type of plant, such as one bucket of strawberries, one bucket of tomatoes, one for cucumbers, and another for a citrus tree. In this way, there is no competition. Of course, you also have to have plants on the same water pump and timer as outlined in water maintenance.

Growing Medium Options

You should make sure you get the correct growing medium as well for every single plant that you're maintaining. Rockwool, expanded clay aggregate, coconut fibers, and even oasis are all different materials that work better as a growing medium than others for various plants. You should take all of these into consideration for every single plant so you're getting the yield that you want without too many problems.

Ideally, when starting off and when expanding your garden, you should use a high quality medium to give yourself the best start for any new plant, or some expanding plants. Mediums like gravel, sand, peat moss, expanded clay, and composted bark will work for many of the plants.

You should also shy away from using certain vermiculite for your plants, and for a good reason. This is a substance that can be risky for not only the health of the plant, but yours as well. This substance might seem harmless, but the fibers do contain asbestos, and these are very dangerous for your respiratory health and your overall health. You should avoid using this at all costs, and do make sure that if it does contain any of this substance, it isn't used. Not all vermiculite is the same; however, if you buy cheap and you do not read the package, you may end up with some that contains asbestos. This is why you should avoid using the product at all, given that you may never be certain whether it contains asbestos or not.

Important Maintenance Tips

Now, when you have a garden, it's important that you make sure that it's maintained correctly. If you're not taking care of the garden, it will suffer. There are a couple of different elements to keep in mind so you can have the best, most successful garden imaginable.

Hydroponic gardens may not contain soil, but this does not mean pests cannot affect your plants. You can still find disease and pests affecting the growth of the plant, the fruit or vegetable, or the overall health of the plant. There are ways to ensure the pests and plant disease do not wreak havoc in your garden.

- Keep the environment clean: remove any dust, immediately remove cobwebs, spray around the edges of the room for bugs, but not around the hydroponic system. A clean, well maintained environment will reduce the risk of pests and disease.
- The plants and room need to be properly ventilated. Disease occurs when ventilation is weak or when air particles are introduced that can harm a plant.
- Proper temperature can also lessen the issue with disease. It will not help with pests as many also like warm temperatures.

However, maintaining a plant's temperature at appropriate levels reduces the risk of certain bacteria or mold growth.

- Water, you will see this again and again. The type of water, the water maintenance, pH balance, and circulating water all determine whether a plant is healthy. Stagnant water can breed pests and disease, even things like mold. Letting water stand near the roots can create rot, which creates decay, and leads to plant death. Overwatering can also lead to blight.

You can prevent problems by choosing plants that are hardier. There are certain plants that are harder to kill for any gardener. These plants tend to have low maintenance requirements. Once you succeed with hardy plants, you can move on to the more fragile plant and attempt to grow it in your hydroponic system. As you grow your plants, you will want to monitor leaf health, stalk health, veggie or fruit health, and growth. If at any stage of the plant's development there looks like disease or pests are hurting your plant, then you can handle it accordingly.

Pruning for Plant Maintenance

You should also prune regularly. It was started in a previous chapter that vegetables do need it to prevent root tangling and messes, but you should make sure to prune every single plant to help with the growing environment. You should use a pair of clean scissors that are sharp, and take them to the chewed leaves or leaves that are looking like they have a disease. You should also get rid of any diseased sections and any roots that might be suffering. This will allow the plants to be fuller, and to use the emery to create more shoots and allow you to yield more crop in your hydroponic garden. You can also purchase pruning shears. You definitely want something that is sharp and that will make a quick cut. Tearing the plant leaves or stems with dull shears can lead to plant death.

Tips on Lighting

If you're looking for good lights, do take a look at the various types of them. Typically, metal halide is a red spectrum lighting, which is good for plants that need a red hue wave length. In contrast, the high pressure sodium lights are a lighting system that's great for older, more mature plants to help them continue on living. LEDs are the third type of lighting that can be helpful in your hydroponic garden, but they do tend to be slightly more expensive. You will see better growth with LED lights, plus you have the ability to change the power to help control plant growth. These are the three best types of lights available for hydroponic gardens.

Adding nutrients

When it comes to adding nutrients, there are some that work better than others. For every single plant, nutrients are required, in order to get the best growth possible. There are some micronutrients and macro-nutrients that you must keep in mind and apply to your garden in order to have the best possible outcome for your plant.

The essential macro-nutrients are boron, copper, cobalt, iron, and zinc, and you should make sure that the medium has enough of those by using the proper growing measurements. Along with this, you should also take the time to make sure the pH is at the right level for the plants. It all depends on the type of plants that you have been growing.

When it comes to other macro-nutrients, there are also some that should be in trace amounts, especially since these are important for plant growth. These are typically there already, but if it's not enough, you should implement a means to have them in the nutrient solution.

- For example, nitrogen is used to help with the growth of the foliage and should be there.

- Phosphorus is needed for root growth, and if your plant blooms, it will need that.

- If your plants are prone to getting sick, you should increase the potassium to help fight off the disease and to generate a higher resistance.

- Calcium allows the plant to have new shoots and roots as well to help it grow and expand.

- Magnesium helps increase the chlorophyll for a plant and to make it produce more food. This is good for any plants that need a bit of a boost in their plant food production.

Ideally, you should keep all of these in mind and test your medium frequently so that it has the right nutrients within it. There are two popular solutions, you can consider making at home. These nutrient solutions have been around for ages.

Nutrient Formula 1

1-ounce ammonium nitrate, calcium sulfate and potassium sulfate.

0.5-ounce magnesium sulfate and diammonium phosphate.

You would need a 10-gallon reservoir for these amounts.

Nutrient Formula 2

1-ounce sodium nitrate, calcium nitrate, potassium sulfate.

0.5-ounce magnesium sulfate

1.5-ounces single super phosphate

Again you would require 10 gallons of water for the mixture.

To add the trace elements, you can use ½ tsp of manganese chloride and zinc sulfate, 1.25 tsp boric acid powder, 1/5 tsp copper sulfate and 2 tsp iron chelate and mix it in 1 gallon of water. You would then allow the two mixtures to combine in the reservoir. You can also spray the trace elements over the plants independently.

All of these tips will allow you to grow your plants easily and without too many issues. Growing a hydroponic garden can take work when you first start, but once you read these tips and implement them, you will definitely grow the plants that you want to, and you'll be able to be successful with your hydroponic garden endeavors no matter what they are.

Chapter 10: Common Mistakes Newbies Make

It is very exciting to think you will soon have your own hydroponics garden, whether it is in a greenhouse, a room of your home, or outside. You are anxious to get started. You feel you have read dozens upon dozens of words about creating your system and how to grow the fruits, vegetables, and herbs. But, you are not quite ready to begin. You want hydroponics to be fun and rewarding, which means you need to effectively manage your garden and avoid these 11 common mistakes. These mistakes are in some ways related to the troubleshooting chapter because there can be errors within your system that need correction; however, they are also things you, as a human might cause, which you have to fix before you can troubleshoot your gardening system.

Starting Your Garden without Proper Knowledge

Any hobby requires knowledge. Sometimes you can learn as you enjoy your hobby, but for hydroponic gardening, you will discover more fun and enjoyment if you arm yourself with the proper education first. A lot of novice gardeners start out without gathering all the information required to start, which can lead to issues with the system or proper nutrient dispersal. You have started out well by reading this book, but if there are fruits and vegetables not mentioned in the commonly grown plant section, then you will want to do more research.

Harvesting too Early

Each plant has its own harvesting time table. A few plants will go from seed to plant to full fruit or vegetable in as little as a month. Other plants can take 70 to 120 days from germination to harvest time. It would be nice if you can start picking fruits and vegetables off the plants as soon as they appear, but you risk an immature vegetable or fruit, which can mean a poor taste. Let the fruits and vegetables grow to full maturity before picking them.

Overwatering/Under Watering

Water is a crucial element to growing your plants; however, there is a fine line between not watering enough and watering too much. The reason hydroponic systems need to have a timer is so you can regulate the watering process with more accuracy. Continually saturating the plants with water will create drooping leaves, as well as hinder the growth of the plants. Some plants will start to rot due to too much water. You also cannot let the roots get too dry. Dry roots mean not enough nutrients, plus they will shrivel up and die. A good rule of thumb is to water your plants when you see the top layer of medium become dry. Stick your finger into the medium and test whether it is wet. If it is not, then you are not watering your plants enough. Other reasons to set up your hydroponic system with drainage is to ensure your plants are not over watered. The roots can soak up what they need and the rest of the water will go back into the reservoir.

Improper Lighting

Even the best gardeners know that sometimes daylight just is not enough because it can be infrequent. The sun might be behind a cloud or it might be raining, which takes away from the proper light required for your crops. For your crop to grow to its proper height and to keep the leaves a healthy green, you have to provide proper light. Reading lights and single bulbs are not the best lamps, which most novices tend to use. Fluorescent bulbs can be okay, but they are highly expensive to run and replace. This is why it is suggested to avoid the mistake of regular lights and fluorescent bulbs in favor of using high pressure sodium or LED lights, which are more cost effective. It does not mean plants need light 24/7, but consistent light without overheating the plant is necessary.

Ignoring pH

The hydroponic system works on pH regulation. New gardeners tend to do well at first with proper monitoring of pH, but once the novelty wears off, so does the time one pays to monitoring the pH. The nutrient solution needs to be monitored for a balanced pH, which may vary depending on the plants you are growing. You can buy equipment to help you adjust the pH. When growing different plants, it is easy to make mistakes on the pH because plants tend to need different degrees of acidic levels. For example, beans require a pH of 6 to 6.5, while cabbage is best grown in 6.5 to 7.5. Pineapple is on the other end of the scale at 5 to 5.5 pH. With hydroponic systems when the pH rises above 6.5, there are some nutrients and micro-nutrients that precipitate out of the nutrient solution. This means the nutrients remain in the reservoir or growing chambers, rather than reaching the plant roots. Iron is one mineral that will precipitate out at 7.3 and at 8 pH there is no more iron. A plant deficiency in nutrients means poor fruit or worse plant death.

Overfeeding the Plants

Like overwatering, anything can be done in excess. Providing fertilizer to your plants; particularly, in a hydroponic system, can be overdone. You could add too many salt deposits or create a fungus issue in the medium, which leads to stunted growth. Hydroponic fertilizer is the nutrient solution, which is combined with water, so if you are over watering, you may also be over fertilizing your plants. Hydroponic fertilizer is usually made with salts, such as potassium chloride. However, the chlorine can actually become harmful to your plants if you apply it for more than two or three days. Magnesium nitrate is another option, which is basically Epsom salts. The main ingredients of your hydroponic garden solution do need to be nitrogen, phosphorus and potassium, you also need trace amounts of iron, sulfur, zinc, manganese, boron, copper, magnesium, chlorine, calcium, and molybdenum. If you are not buying a premade nutrient solution, then study before you start to make your own to ensure you have the proper amount of all nutrients.

Insufficient Air Circulation

Another common mistake is not providing the proper ventilation your plants need to remain healthy. This does not mean you need to infuse the water with oxygen, but rather allow plenty of air into the grow room. Monitoring humidity and oxygen quality in the grow room will ensure you are providing proper air circulation for better plant health. You may need to have a blower or fan in the area. Make sure that none of your plants are directly in the path of the fan, blower, or air conditioning vent as this can make them cold and dormant.

Unhygienic Conditions

Hydroponic growing systems still need maintenance, as you learned in an earlier chapter. One of the most common mistakes new plant growers make is to leave the dead plant matter or debris in the grow room. Wet floors, non-sterile equipment, and an unprotected solution tank can cause problems, such as bacterial build up. Your reservoir tank might develop mold, algae, or a layer of dust film that interferes with proper health of your plant. You will need to keep things clean and dust free to keep your plants healthy.

Falling into the Cheap Trap

Anything labeled "plant food" might be something you think you need, but it rarely is. Hydroponic gardens are much different than soil gardens. You already learned about pH, proper nutrients, and air circulation, so you need to keep these things in mind when you visit a store. Going into a warehouse style store that sells anything and everything does not mean you need their plant food. Most people working in the gardening section have minimal training versus a plant dedicated store that specifically hires experts to work there. Asking for advice about the nutrients and fertilizers to purchase is good, but do not stop there. Ask why one brand is better than another or why they made that recommendation, so you can understand how it will work in your hydroponic garden. Purchasing seeds, plants, fertilizer, nutrients, and even hydroponic systems for cheap or through unauthorized dealers can lead to dead plants, foliage damage, and plant disease that kills your entire garden. To have a sustainable garden, you cannot make the mistake of starting off with ill or nearly dead plants. You will have a losing battle each time if you go cheap on the plants.

Pest Control via Plants

Later you will learn about three measures you can use for pest control. However, there is also a common mistake many make when it comes to protecting their gardens from pests. They forget that there are natural methods that include actual plants. Garlic is one form of pest control. Adding this to an outdoor garden will help keep pests from coming to investigate the rest of your garden. Coffee grinds are another form of natural pest control. Dried coffee is a pesticide for most bugs that will eat your plants. You can sprinkle grinds around your buckets or the bottoms of the hydroponic system to prevent pests from crawling into the medium and up the plant. You do not want to use it on top of the medium as this would affect pH levels, which is also a common mistake for hydroponic newbies. Some already know coffee grinds are great for pests and put it in the medium like it is soil, thus contaminating their system.

Chapter 11: Troubleshooting Your Hydroponics Garden

Growing plants hydroponically is an art. Because you do not have the same set up as you would with a traditional garden, you are responsible for providing your plants with the light, water, and nutrients that they need to grow. Sometimes, however, our systems do not allow our plants to flourish as we intended. In these cases, the first step is to check for common problems in the system. Once you locate what is wrong, you will be able to fix your hydroponic system so that it grows larger, better harvests.

Troubleshooting Issue #1: The Lighting

Whether you are using natural or artificial lighting, there are a few things to consider in regards to how well your plants are growing.

Natural Lighting

When it comes to natural lighting, you should ask yourself:

- Is the plant getting enough natural light? If you are growing inside, be sure the window that your plant is sitting in gets an adequate amount of light during the day. If you are growing outside, make sure the area your plants are in is not covered by shade too much during the day.

- Are you growing out of season? If the daylight is shorter or the shading is different depending on the time of year, you may want to switch to artificial lighting.

- Should you switch to artificial lighting to speed up the growth of your plant? When you use artificial light, you have more control over grow cycles and you can reap more harvests.

Artificial Lighting

- Are you using the right kind of lights? Most fluorescent lights are not compatible with growing plants. You should be using HID lights.

- How close or far away from the plant is the light? Your light should be no lower than 1 foot away, but no higher than 2 feet. Adjust according to the size of your hydroponics garden. You should also adjust the wattage to a higher number of watts the farther you are from the plant.

- Are my plants getting too hot to grow? The simplest way to see if your plants are too hot (your bulb is too close) is to put your hand just above your plants. If it gets hot, then you need to move the light further away. You can also keep a thermometer under the light, close to the plants to test the temperature near your plants, versus the overall room temperature.

Troubleshooting Issue #2: The Growing Climate

If the climate is not right, your plants will not be able to grow. Be sure that you take the specific needs of the plant in mind and adjust the moisture level and temperature accordingly.

- Is the temperature of your growing system between 60 degrees and 90 degrees? You should also make sure that the temperature drops by 10 degrees at night, as this is important for the night/day rhythm of the growing cycle

- Is the air being properly ventilated? The last thing that you want is to have an excess of stale air around your plants. You should install a vent or even a fan, so that the leaves are gently stirred around throughout the day and night.

- Is the relative humidity of the growing area between 50 percent and 70 percent? This is considered safest for growing, because too much humidity can interfere with growing processes and encourage the growth of mold. Between 50 and 60%, is the most optimal range of humidity, but as much as 70% is acceptable for certain plants.

Troubleshooting Issue #3: The Nutrient System

In regards to the nutrient system, here is what you should ask:

- Is there enough solution in the reservoir? If your pump is sucking any air during the cycles, then it is likely you need to add more nutrient solution to your reservoir.

- Do you have an adequate ratio of water to nutrients? If you think that the concentration of your solution is the problem, discard the entire batch and start over.

- Is the temperature of the reservoir below 85 degrees? Keeping the temperature under 80 is preferred, but under 85 is adequate.

- Is the pH of the nutrient system balanced? Check the pH of your nutrient solution regularly to be sure that your plants are getting what they need. If you need to raise or lower the pH, there are drops that you can buy to do this.

Troubleshooting Issue #4: Pests

It can be hard to pinpoint the reason for pests to show up on your hydroponic garden, especially if you have used sterile buckets and nutrient mixture. However, it does sometimes happen and when it does, you need to use one of the following three options.

Hand-Pick the Bugs Off

If you catch bugs early on, this is the most effective way to get rid of them. Pick the pests off by hand and put them in a container (you can release them or kill them). Do this for a few days until you notice that there are no bugs remaining.

Take Advantage of Natural Predators

If you have a screened in porch, or if you are growing your hydroponic garden outside, you may be able to use bugs to get rid of your pests. Bugs like lacewings and ladybugs have voracious appetites when it comes to "bad" plant bugs like mealybugs and aphids. This is obviously a method that you do not want to use for your indoor setup, but it is extremely effective (and safe) for biological pest control.

Last Resort-Organic Pesticides

If you are like most people, then one of the reasons you are growing hydroponic fruits, vegetables, and herbs is because you do not want dangerous chemicals and pesticides in your fruit. Unless you want to throw away your entire crop because of a bug infestation; however, it may end up being your only option. The first thing that you must do is identify the bugs that are on your plant. If you go with an organic pesticide, the ingredients are more likely to target a specific type of bug than be a one-size-fits all solution. Then, look for organic pesticides that will not leave a harmful residue on your crops. Here are a few tips:

- Look for non-toxic pesticides. These are going to be the safest for your plants (and you!).

- Follow the instructions closely. Pesticides that are non-toxic may take several applications before all of the bugs can be exterminated.

- To prevent the artificial or natural light from harming your plants, spray the pesticides in the evening. This will allow them to dry so your plants do not burn.

- If you do have to use pesticides, be sure to stop spraying at least one week before you harvest the plant. Additionally, wash before you eat.

Identifying Critters

There are a number of things that can indicate an oncoming critter infestation, including icky coatings, discoloration, and more. Here are the most common bug signs and how you can get rid of them.

- Webs- If you see the webs on your plants, then spider mites are a likely culprit. Spider mites are red, but very small, so unless you are looking for them or you have a large infestation, they are hard to see. In addition to webs, you will probably notice yellowish-white specks on the leaves of your plant. This is caused by the spider mites sucking out the plant fluids. Eventually, this will turn brown unless you take care of the problem. You may also notice the eggs of spider mites, which are small and round. They are also translucent, with a white to amber color.

    - If you catch the infestation early on, you may be able to get rid of mites by raising the humidity and temperature. Because spider mites prefer dry, cool conditions, doing this may send them packing.

    - If that does not work, consider investing in predator mites. These are the natural enemy of spider mites and you will need to purchase one predator mite to every 100 spider mites that you believe you have.

    - If you must resort to using chemicals, be sure that you are purchasing a blend made with Neem Oil. You can also consider using Neem Oil by itself, though it may not be quite as efficient as the pesticide.

- Wilted, sickly plants- If you have noticed that your plants have almost stopped growing, or that they are sickly or wilted in appearance, aphids may be to blame. If you do not resolve this problem, the plants will turn brown and curl inward. This is because aphids suck the sap out of the leaves and also have saliva that is toxic to plants and often filled with disease. If you inspect the underside of the plant, you will find dense, yellowish areas. These are softer-bodied bugs that are known as aphids. Another thing to be wary of is ants- aphids let off a sticky honeydew trail that is very tasty to ants.

    o These are a bug that you can hunt and pick off, especially because they often hang out in such dense colonies. They may be on the undersides of leaves, but also on the tips. Crush them as you pick them off.

    o There are a number of bugs that prey on aphids. Some good choices include green lacewings, ladybugs, and gall midges.

    o Neem oil is also effective against aphids. Find a pesticide that includes this ingredient.

- Cotton-like substance in crooks of leaves- If you have cotton-like substances on your plant, then it is likely mealybugs. Mealybugs have the appearance of cotton, especially when they group together in colonies. Your leaves will become distorted and your plants can become weak, often dying quickly.

    o This is a bug that is particularly difficult to battle using the pick-and-remove method. You may be able to win if you catch the infestation very early, but you will need a great amount of vigilance.

- o For biological warfare, introduce a couple of ladybugs into the growing environment. Lady bugs find mealybugs to be a tasty treat!

- o Neem oil can be effective, so look for a pesticide with this ingredient. You will likely need several applications to get rid of this pest.

- Whitish-yellow spots with a metallic sheen- If you have whitish-yellow spots appearing on your plants, then thrips may be to blame. These are small wormy-looking creatures with legs. If you do not get the infestation under control, your plants will eventually turn brittle. You may also notice black dots, which are thrip feces. Shake a branch and you should see the critters start running. Here is how to deal with them:

  - o In order to locate the thrips, shake the leaves. Then, pick up the bugs and squish them. In the early stages of an infestation, you will be able to kill them by hand.

  - o There are a number of bugs that can help with biological warfare, including green lacewings, parasitic wasps, and predatory mites.

  - o You will definitely want to treat these with a specific pesticide if they get too severe.

Troubleshooting Issue #5: Gross Coatings (Not From Bugs)

Sometimes, you may notice gross coatings on your plants. The first step to treating the issue is to find out exactly what you are dealing with.

Gray Mold

Gray mold is soot-like in color and can also have tints of white. It may even look like lint, or hair. Gray mold is the most common cause of extra humidity. Once this mold gets hold of your plants, it can become fatal very quickly. If you can catch it early, however, you may have a fighting chance. Here's how:

- Begin by taking a soft, dry cloth and use it to gently remove the mold from the leaves of your plant.

- Look closely at the growing material. If you see any dead debris or matter, remove it. These can become candidates for mold growth.

- To prevent more growth, immediately increase the circulation and ventilation in your growing area and decrease the level of humidity in the room.

Tobacco Mosaic Virus

Tobacco mosaic virus will cause your plants to die. Plants like tomatoes, cucumbers, and peppers are especially susceptible to contracting this disease. The best thing to do in this case is to prevent the tobacco mosaic virus in the first place, because it can be very dangerous to your plants. Here is what to do for prevention:

- Do not smoke in your growing room. Do not let anyone else smoke in your hydroponic growing room either.

- If at all possible, do not let someone who smokes handle your plants. If you cannot avoid it, be sure that the smoker washes their hands thoroughly using hot water and antibacterial soap. This may not even prevent it, but this is your best bet.

Damping Off

Damping off is a disease that affects new seedlings and there is no cure once it takes hold. After your plant is affected, it will collapse and fall over, dead. Fortunately, you can take the following measure for prevention.

- Make sure that the planting material you choose is sterile and fast draining.

- Routinely apply an all-purpose fungicide to your plant area.

Powdery Mildew

Powdery mildew appears as white spots that covers the tops of leaves early on. As the mildew progresses, it turns into a gray-white powder that covers the entire plant. This will cause the growth of your plant to slow down, and eventually die. Fortunately, powdery mildew is one of the less serious diseases. It can be treated using the same measures that you would use for prevention.

- Decrease the amount of humidity that is in your growing environment

- Increase the amount of light intensity (make sure your plants are not getting too hot, though!)

- Increase the ventilation and air circulation

- Regularly apply an all-purpose fungicide

Wilt Diseases

There are two different wilt diseases that can affect your plant- Fusarium Wilt and Verticullum Wilt. These will start as small spots on eggplants, peppers, and tomatoes. Then, the leaves that are on the lower part of the plants are going to wilt and the plant will die. In order to prevent this (there is no treatment), take the following steps:

- Buy tomatoes that are resistant to wilt. These will be labeled as V or F type.

- Always start with fresh and clean growing medium- never reuse the material from a previous harvest.

- Make sure you are disinfecting your reservoir, growing chamber, pipes, and any other materials between harvests.

Algae

Algae is one of the safer coatings that you will find on your plants. It appears as a greenish colored guck over the top of your planting media, and possibly in your nutrient reservoir. While algae are relatively safe, you should still take its presence as a warning. It shows that conditions like humidity, excessive water and light, and stagnant water may be present, all of which can lead to more serious plant diseases. To treat algae, do the following:

- If your growing medium is porous, put one to two inches of leca stones on top of your pot. This will create a dry barrier between your plants and the growing medium.

- Scrape any visible algae off.

- Correct the conditions that are causing your algae to prevent the growth of this and other diseases in the future.

Tips for Preventing Gross Coatings

The two primary causes of icky coatings on your hydroponic plants are stale air and humidity. To help stop mold, algae, and other coatings, follow these tips:

- Use an air conditioner to regulate the temperature of your growing room.

- Keep a fan running at all times. Your goal should be to keep your leaves rustling slowly.

- It is important that you do not over-water your plants. This can make the growing material excessively wet and encourage the growth of mold, mildew, and fungus.

- Do not reuse your growing material and nutrient solution. Also, use a solution of ten parts water to one-part bleach to clean your set up between harvests.

- Use opaque coating and tubing so that light is not seeping into your system and encouraging unwanted growths.

Troubleshooting Issue #6: The Leaves

One of the best indicators that there is something wrong with your hydroponic plants or even your growing system is the leaves of your plants. If you know what to look for, you can easily learn of disease, pests, climate issues, and nutrient deficiencies early on- before your plants are not able to be saved. In this section, you will learn what to look for.

Integrity of the Leaves

- Wilted leaves- Wilting leaves can be an indication of a simple growing problem, such as over-watering, under-watering, or an environment that is too hot or dry. When leaves wilt and curl up or dry out, it can be an indication of something more serious, like Wilt Disease.

- Curled up leaves- If your leaves are curling up, then aphids or thrips may be to blame. Check for these critters using the tips in the bug infestation section.

- Drooping leaves- When your leaves start to drop, there are a few problems that may be at hand. The temperature may be too high, or your plant may not be getting enough fluids. It is also possible that you are giving your plants too much nutrient solution, in which case you should flush the system (and your plants with water for 1 week before starting a new mixture of nutrient solution.

- Distorted or crinkly leaves- This could be an indication of aphids, or one of several viruses. Check for other symptoms to more specifically diagnose your plant.

- Dropping leaves- If your leaves are falling, then a sudden temperature change or another kind of shock may to be blame. It can also be caused by over watering and exposure to cold wind or excessively dry air. As far as insects, it could also indicate mealybugs.

Discoloration

- Yellowing is an indication of a nutrient imbalance or overwatering. It can also be an indication of whiteflies. Plant leaves can also turn yellow when they are at the end of their lifecycle, so know when to uproot the plants and start over.

- Browning of leaf tips- If your leaf tips are turning brown, it could be too much nutrient solution. Flush with water for a week before resuming with a new batch of nutrient solution. Your leaves may also turn brown if they burn, which can be caused by hot, dry air or the light source being too close.

Other Troubleshooting Problems

While we have covered some of the main issues you will have so far, keep your eye out for the common problems in this section as well.

Seedling Issues

There are two major issues that happen with seedlings. The first is damping off, which is addressed earlier in this chapter. The second is spindly growth, which occurs when your seedlings are really thin and tall. This problem is caused by not having enough light. The plants overstretch as they try to grow toward the light source and overstretching causes them to become spindly.

Conclusion

Now that you know all about hydroponic gardens, you can see that it's not something crazy when you look at it. You should make sure that you take care of it. As long as you know what you're doing when you're growing your garden you will succeed. It will take time, but once you start to grow these plants in your hydroponic garden, you'll be able to get the benefits from hydroponics.

Think about it, with this garden, you can get all of the foods that you love, and you can certainly enjoy these benefits for a lifetime. Plus, maintaining and growing a hydroponic garden is fun, although challenging at times, and it gives you benefits that you might have never expected to achieve until now.

With that being said, the next thing that you should do is get the materials together and plan your hydroponic garden. Do take everything said here in mind before you get started so you have a surefire plan, but once you do get started, everything will fall into place. So do that, work on your garden, and achieve the success you desire.

I hope you were able to find out everything you wanted to know about a hydroponic garden. If you have any questions, feel free to let me know. I hope your experiences with this amazing and intriguing gardening system which spans over many different areas, helps you get results from your garden that are better than anything you've expected before.

-- Michael Martinez

Special Invitation!

If you liked what you read and would like to read high quality books, get free bonuses, and get notified first of **FREE EBOOKS,** then join the official Xcension Publishing Company Book Club! Membership is free, but space is limited!

You can join the Book Club by visiting the link below:

http://www.xcensionpublishing.com/book-club

Made in the USA
San Bernardino, CA
28 September 2018